Little Things Mean A Lot

Other Books by Susan Newman

Little Things Mean A Lot

Creating
Happy Memories with Your
Grandchildren

Susan Newman, Ph.D.

Illustrations by Cary McIver

Crown Publishers, Inc.
New York

Published by Crown Publishers, Inc.,
201 East 50th Street, New York, New York 10022.
Member of the Crown Publishing Group.

Random House, Inc. New York, Toronto, London, Sydney, Auckland
www.randomhouse.com

CROWN and colophon are trademarks of Crown Publishers, Inc.

Printed in the United States of America

Design by Mercedes Everett

Library of Congress Cataloging-in-Publication Data
Newman, Susan.
  Little things mean a lot : creating happy memories with your
  grandchildren / by Susan Newman.—1st ed.
  1. Grandparenting—Miscellanea. 2. Grandparent and child—
  Miscellanea. I. Title.
HQ759.9.N49   1996   306.874'5—dc20   96–1931

ISBN 0-517-70463-3

10 9 8 7 6 5

In loving memory of Grandma Anita.

With warm thanks to Grandpa Irving, Aunt Mae, and

Grandma Toni, for the memories they so abundantly create,

and to grandchildren Andrew, Nina, Courtney, and Meagan,

who explained their grandparents' love and unique traditions.

Contents

Little Things Mean A Lot

The Grandparent Credo

Grandparents give time.

Grandparents give love.

Grandparents give gifts.

Grandparents think big.

Grandparents are good sports.

Grandparents are patient and understanding.

*Grandparents are always supportive and
enthusiastic.*

*Grandparents pass on tradition and share their
history.*

*Grandparents don't disagree with parents in front
of grandchildren.*

*Grandparents don't interfere with the upbringing of
grandchildren.*

Grandparents are devoted to their grandchildren.

Grandparents are fun.

Grandparents are indispensable.

The Grandparent Connection

From the very first time you hold your grandchild until he or she marries and beyond, everything you do with and for your grandchild makes your bond stronger. The simplest of pleasures will delight both of you and bring you closer together. You'll repeat much of what you discover in this book many times over in the years to come.

The best part of being a grandparent is giving—be it your love, gifts, time, or instruction. You may not realize it just yet, but you have a lot to pass on to the youngest family members. Your grandchildren will delight in your stories, listen to your warnings, and love you unconditionally. And you'll experience a new and glorious realm of feelings.

For some grandparents, having a grandchild gives them the opportunity to do many things that they couldn't afford or didn't have the time for as parents. No matter how many grandchildren you have, you have more time to spend than their parents. And surprisingly, no matter how little time you think you have, you'll find the time to let your grandchildren know how special they are to you.

By definition, grandparents have a job: to make the

next generation—your children's children—feel loved, adored, and cherished. What follows are hundreds of ways to capture their hearts and recognize them so they feel important every single day of their lives. It's your latest and most important role in life, second only to raising your own children.

Being a *great* grandparent is a delicious, rewarding experience. Ultimately you decide what you mean to your grandchildren by how you embrace them in your heart and show your love. That's the genuine grandparent connection.

Building Bonds

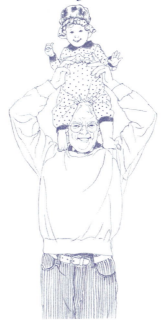

Take advantage of every chance to connect with your grandchildren. You'll find and create endless opportunities to please them, from infancy through the teen years and beyond. Building bonds regularly tells grandchildren you care about and love them. You're the best substitute for Mom or Dad they will ever have, but if you think a parent may want—or want to share—the joy of introducing a child to something, be sure to discuss the new activity with the parent first.

Too Bumpy

That's almost never the case when you give your grandchildren piggyback rides. For them, the rides are always too short.

Being There

If you live close to your grandchild, try to be at his house when he returns from school if his parent can't.

Count on Me

Stand in for an unavailable parent when your grandchild has a dental or doctor's appointment.

The Big Squeeze

Provide bear hugs whenever you meet.

The Little Squeeze

Pinch those adorable cheeks every chance you get. Too soon, your grandchildren will be embarrassed by this "grandparently" expression of love.

Between Us

Find a word or phrase that makes the baby laugh and repeat it every time you're together. She'll always associate that word or expression with you.

Naming Names

You may have the luxury of choosing what you would like your grandchildren to call you. Pick carefully, because once adopted, you'll probably be stuck with it.

His Choice

If your grandchild comes up with a name for you—Grammy, Pop Pop—don't try to change it. He's picked one he feels comfortable with.

Princess Popcorn

Devise an affectionate, clever name for each grandchild. Whether it's "Handsome Harry," "Miss Muffin," or "Frannie Fab," its regular use will become part of family lore.

Barrel Full

Arrive with (or send) a bucket of pretzels or popcorn. The container can be used after it's empty to hold toys and "things."

Louder

Sing songs together—the sillier and louder, the more fun you'll all have.

Loving Reminders

An occasional call just to say "I love you" reminds grandchildren that they are very special.

Pickup

Surprise your grandchild by picking him up alone (or with his mother or father) after school.

Ryan, Joel, Josh, and Ben

Pay attention to the names of your grandchild's friends. Ask about them and use their names in conversation frequently.

Not Out of Mind

Send home a silver dollar or fifty-cent piece to the grandchild who couldn't visit to let her know you are thinking about her.

Very Funny

Share a joke (age-appropriate, of course). Make it a habit to have a new joke or riddle ready whenever you call or visit.

Just Talk

Grandchildren appreciate having someone who will listen to them. Pay close attention to your young "talker."

School Days

Ask lots of questions about school. Remind your grandchild that getting an education is his top priority; it's his job. He'll probably take the advice better from you than he would from a parent.

Rover, Bandit, or Max

When a grandchild is naming a new pet, offer suggestions and comment favorably on the names she comes up with.

Can We Play . . .?

Introduce your grandchild to different games. Certain ones will become grandparent/grandchild staples that will be well worn and played with you when a grandchild is in his teens—and older.

Would You?

To make your grandchild feel useful, ask for help even if you don't need it.

Mighty Might

Give it a fun, cheerful name—Super Boy, Dyno Debbie, or Wonder Girl—to call for kid power whenever you really need a grandchild to carry the groceries, retrieve something from another room, or assist you in any way.

Thank You

Always thank your grandchild when he assists you in whatever way that may be.

Conversation Starters

Find out what your grandchildren are interested in or what events are upcoming *before* you visit.

One for You, One for Me

Whenever possible, make a copy of her "good" drawings while your grandchild is still with you so she knows you think her work is excellent.

Stargazing

Sit on the porch and point out the constellations.

Helping

Involve your grandchild in any volunteer or charity work you might do. If she can't tag along with you, be sure to tell her all about the good work you do and how it benefits others.

Corporate Image

If your company or volunteer organization has hats, mugs, T-shirts, or other items with the group's logo, be sure to give one to your grandchild.

Men's Morning Out
Take your grandson for a haircut.

Keep Those Cards and Letters Coming
You live around the corner. It doesn't matter. Children love mail. Send note cards with interesting pictures (preprinted, drawn, or cut out and pasted on), a sheet of paper folded a peculiar way, or one cut into puzzle pieces for them to arrange in order to read your message.

Congratulations by Mail
Send short congratulatory postcards or letters.

Funny Funnies
Mail a cartoon that relates to something the two of you have discussed or that you think your grandchild will find amusing.

On-line
Even if you live nearby, technological grandparents send mail on-line daily to grandchildren. The computer provides a great way to keep up-to-date on schoolwork, accomplishments, and interests. It's especially effective for keeping in contact with older grandchildren.

Encourage Calling

Give responsible older grandchildren telephone calling cards to be used only to call you. Calling cards can be restricted to certain telephone numbers. (Clear with parents first.)

This Little Piggy

Give your grandchild a starter piggy bank and remember to offer pennies now and then for feeding to the "pig."

Portfolio

Even if your grandchild's stock holdings are a share or two, discuss buying and selling as you would with major investments.

Are You Okay?

Young grandchildren work hard and laugh hard as they attempt to roll Grandma or Grandpa off a couch or bed.

Wrong, Again

Be a joker. Grandchildren love it when you consistently mispronounce a word—"sign-on-men" for cinnamon or "hamsmurger" for hamburger.

Planned Confusion

Most older grandchildren find it amusing when you mix up their boyfriends' (James for John) and girlfriends' (Hillary and Heather) names—never in front of the friend, of course!

Slide Down

Share a sled down a steep, steep hill.

After the Fall

Point out branch patterns after the leaves have fallen from the trees. Look for interesting designs together.

Agile, Still

Climb a tree with your grandchild.

Faster, Please

Ride a go-cart with your grandchild.

How Terrible

Take your grandchild's complaints and problems seriously. Be very sympathetic.

Be Understanding

There are times your grandchildren will prefer their parents. Don't take it personally.

You're Terrific

Seize every opportunity to tell your grandchild how great you think she is.

Good to Remember

Here's a short list of expressions to praise your grandchild that you will want to memorize and say

(with an exclamation in your voice) whenever you
you have the opportunity:

* good job
* you're the greatest
* masterful
* right on
* knew you could do it

* good thinking
* you're wonderful
* superb
* perfect
* nice going

Long-distance "Little Things"

You can stay close no matter how far away you live. You'll make your presence known in ways so simple that they'll become automatic. Small gestures frequently are the most meaningful. Here, simple suggestions for the times you can't be physically present.

Once a Month

Put your grandchild on the mailing list for magazines geared to his age group and special interest. Each month when a new issue arrives, he'll be reminded of you. There are many magazines from which to choose and ones to satisfy all kinds of curiosities—from computers and humor to sports. Change subscriptions as your grandchild outgrows a current passion.

Any Mail for Me?

Stuff a dollar or two in an envelope and mail it off to your grandchild with instructions to use it to buy or save for something she would like.

Is My Grandchild There?

Call solely to speak with your grandchild. Hang up immediately after your conversation, no matter how brief. Call another time of day to speak with his parents.

Techno-Savvy

Take advantage of technology. Send your grandchild a fax just for him. Fax a photo you think your grandchild might like. Or send a hand-drawn heart with an "I love you" or "I miss you" message.

Postcards from Everywhere

Send postcards whenever you travel.

Postcards from Nowhere

You don't have to go anywhere to keep your grandchild "in mail." Send a postcard from a local restaurant, art gallery, or hotel.

Thirsty

Send a note or small surprise in a water bottle. Attach the mailing label right on the outside of the bottle; place the straw inside.

Always There

Give your grandchild a framed picture of you for her dresser or night table.

Who Will Your Teacher Be?

Call the day before school begins each year to show your interest in and support of his schoolwork.

They Liked It, Too

Mail off a movie review of a film you saw with your grandchild.

See This

Send a movie review of a film you think your grandchild would enjoy.

Reach Out and Touch Someone

Call more often than you think you should.

Top of His Game

Call before major sporting events in which your grandchild is competing to wish him good luck.

One-sided Conversations

Record your messages—especially the long ones—on an audiocassette and mail it off to your grandchild to listen to on her or her parents' tape player.

Storytelling from Afar

Read bedtime stories onto an audio (or video) tape and mail it with the book so the child can follow along as she listens to your voice.

Fax for Buildup

Send teasers and information about an upcoming event you plan to share with your grandchild. Ask how many elephants you'll see at the circus. How many tigers at the zoo? How many dancers in the ballet? How many tries will it take to win a stuffed animal at the carnival?

Spelling Fax

Have your grandchild fax you or tell you her weekly spelling words. You can study with her over the phone once you have the list.

Congratulations

Call to congratulate a good test score.

A+

Ask your school-age grandchild to send you class-work or test papers she's proud of. Let her know you plan to hang them on your refrigerator or bulletin board.

Fax Riddle

"What's crunchy, sometimes has bananas and sugar?" "What's black and white and 'read' all over?" You've got the idea. One riddle at a time for younger children; a whole page for the older ones.

We Missed You

Videotape family events they may not have been able to attend because of the distance. As you record, be sure to identify people so that your grandchildren will get to know family members they may not see on a regular basis.

Congratulations

Send flowers to recognize a hard-earned achievement.

After the Fact

If you've visited a place with your grandchild, buy

extra postcards to mail months after the trip to remind him of the fun things you saw and did.

On a Regular Basis

Set a regular time for weekly telephone conversations with your grandchildren. Soon videophones will be commonplace and you'll be able to see them as well as speak with them.

Wall Hanging

Send your grandchild a poster of her favorite rock group or sports star.

To Andrew

If you happen upon a celebrity, be sure to get an autograph for your grandchild.

For Campers Only

There's no such thing as too much mail when a child's off at sleep-away camp. Keep letters brief and mail them in colorful envelopes.

What Did You Get?

His bunkmates will be envious as they watch your grandchild open that surprise package from you.

What you send—from a deck of cards or silly putty to the hottest, most dazzling CD—doesn't matter half as much as the fact that it arrived in a big box.

Spending Money

Slip a few dollars into an envelope and send it off to your camper. There's always a little something to buy on a trip out of camp.

Never Out of Style

Some items are welcome whether sent to camp or home: novelty balls, small games, a jump rope, decorated pencil, magnet, yo-yo, or jacks; basketball, baseball, or football cards for the young collector.

Play It Again, Samantha

Request a phone recital. Listen to whatever song your grandchild is practicing. If time permits, ask her to play or sing it again.

Music to Relax with

An audiotape of the actual recital will allow you to enjoy your grandchild's performance as many times as you like. Ask the child or a parent to record it and mail it to you.

Return Mail

An almost surefire way to receive mail from your grandchild is to send her a self-addressed, stamped postcard with a note requesting specific information: How does your gerbil like its new cage? What are you getting your mother for her birthday? Are you teaching your brother to read? . . .

A Book Is Forever

Send a new book occasionally and don't forget to inscribe it to your grandchild.

Flying in

Come in from out of town to baby-sit while your grandchild's parents go on a vacation.

Sharing

$\mathcal{B}$y now you've probably accumulated more "things" than you have room for, use for, or even want. In your piles and boxes of memorabilia, you'll find items your grandchildren will adore—their mother's favorite (perhaps ragged) stuffed animal, pressed prom corsage, or scrapbook from her teen years.

You're also a storehouse of family traditions and

memories. Share them generously along with your feelings and insights. You'll want to add fresh and exhilarating experiences, too. And after you've shared so many aspects of your life, you may be lucky enough to have a grown grandchild say, "My grandmother is my best friend."

Dress Up

Keep a large carton filled with old clothing, hats, and shoes for grandchildren to don for pretend play when they visit. Have them borrow what they need for parades, costume parties, and parts in plays.

Here If You Need Me

Grandchildren don't know they can call on you for help or that you'll be there to listen unless you tell them.

Dad, the Little Leaguer

Give your grandchildren pictures of their parents as close to their ages as possible. The more outrageous their moms and dads are acting in the pictures, the better. Repeat every year or two or three.

Never Could Ice-skate

Reassure the not-so-great athlete by letting him know that at the same age you, his mom, or dad were not so good at whatever he's attempting.

Family Treasures

Offer grandchildren significant family objects. Stress the importance of how old they are and the history behind them. The range of objects is limitless—a photo of your mother and father or the child's great-grandparents, the key to the family's old cabin in the woods, record albums, your father's saxophone . . .

Tradition

Pass down your children's breakfast dishes, books, blankets, high school letter sweaters, or scrapbooks that you may still have. In doing so, you tell your grandchild a lot about her parents and strengthen close family feelings.

The Winner Is . . .

Ask your grandchild's permission to enter his picture in a photography contest. Then wait and watch for the winners together.

Candy Man

Carry a few pieces of candy or gum in your pocket

or purse for your grandchild to discover. Once a sweet is found, she'll always be looking for it.

Giving Back

If you can part with them, grandchildren love the "art pieces" their parents made during their childhoods: the lopsided vase, the carved bookends, the pottery bowl, or painted tray. Whatever it is, it's sure to become the root of many conversations and perhaps some well-meaning laughs.

Once Upon a Time

Grandparent begins a tale—one sentence or thought; grandchild adds the next idea; grandparent moves the story along; now back to grandchild. Keep rotating until story's end.

Tree Branches

Where does the family come from? Who belongs on the family tree? You may be the only family member who knows about great-grandparents and other ancestors. Share your family history.

First Cousins and Half Brothers

Prepare a family tree. It can be as simple as connecting boxes on a sheet of paper, or as intricate as a

computer-generated design. A hand-drawn tree with family member names inserted on the branches will become a grandchild's treasured map of his roots.

Baker's Delight

If you make cookies and cakes while your grandchild is around, be sure to ask her if she would like to stir the batter and lick the beaters afterwards.

No Nuts

Build a gigantic banana split or sundae together, and then share it.

Number-One Assistant

The youngest of grandchildren can be your "right hand" when preparing meals, if only to beat the eggs, place the chairs around the table, fill the bread basket, or carry a dish to the table.

Half Cup Brown Sugar

Give grandchildren old enough to be interested recipes that have been in the family for decades.

When I Was Your Age

Tell as many interesting stories about yourself as you can recall. It will seem like only yesterday to you,

but to grandchildren such stories seem as if they occurred in the Stone Age.

Before Computers

Chances are your grandchildren will be amazed that you listened to records, not CD's; dialed the telephone instead of pressing buttons; rewrote or typed papers from beginning to end if you made mistakes.

Helping Hand

Your help will be greatly appreciated when it's time for your grandchild to clean his pet's cage, tank, or aquarium.

Over and Over

Be willing to repeat a favorite story or reread a favorite book.

I'd Like You to Meet

Introduce your grandchildren to your friends, especially the fun and/or interesting ones.

Looks Like, Acts Like

Reinforce familial similarities—you smile just like your Aunt Cara; you walk like your Uncle Mark; you joke like Cousin Michael—to remind a child of his ties to family.

The Scarf Goes with Everything

Let your grandchild know that you're using her gift so often, it's wearing out.

Stop, Please

Tickle your grandchild until he begs you to stop.

Instruction

Have your grandchild teach you karate, tae kwon do moves, or dance steps recently learned.

Side by Side

Take advantage of every opportunity to sit close—in the car, watching television, playing a game, working on a puzzle.

Spreading the Knowledge

Discuss politics, the environment, or medical issues with school-age grandchildren.

Wash Day

Assisting a grandparent with the laundry is much more acceptable to a child than doing laundry for Mom and Dad.

Grandpa the Great

Embroider stories of your conquests, adventures, and accomplishments.

Where's Charlie?

Get involved in your grandchild's fantasy play or pretend friends. If he thinks you need to walk slowly so "Charlie" can catch up, by all means comply.

Remember When?

No one tells the story of a grandchild's hilarious episodes or quirky sayings better than a grandparent.

And no one wants to hear them repeated more than the grandchild involved.

Forget the Diet

Join him in eating whatever goody he fancies, even if it's not on your diet.

Watch Me

Spot your grandchild on the seesaw, swing, or slide.

Move the Mouse

Ask your grandchild to show you how to play his latest computer or electronic game. You, too, may get hooked.

On the Big Screen

Watch them drink in the frolic of the latest movie extravaganza. Most "kid" movies are so excellent today that you will enjoy watching them as much as watching your grandchildren absorb the big-screen excitement.

Hold the Butter

Balance a vat of popcorn on your lap to share with your young movie companions.

I Am Cinderella

After a movie or story, ask your grandchild to play the main character.

¿Habla Espanol?

Have some fun with a foreign language. Share key words, phrases, or expressions. *Merci beaucoup.*

Discovered in the Alps

Watch for newspaper stories and magazine articles that your grandchild can use for school reports and projects.

In the Spirit

Share your enthusiasm for a professional team by giving your grandchild the team's pennant for his room, a cap for his head, or a T-shirt for his back.

Know It All

It doesn't take much knowledge to become the authority your grandchild turns to for opinions or advice in a certain area. Let him know that you can supply good information on trains or airplanes, gardening or scientific experiments, building, the weather, mountain climbing, painting, or pottery making.

Jane, Joanna, Jack, and Phil

Create a family song that includes the names of relatives near and far.

Reporting Back

Be sure to share compliments you receive about a grandchild's gift, whether she made it or selected it at the store.

Better in the Retelling

Embellish family stories. Tales of what their parents did at their age enrapture young children. They'll realize quickly that they are not so different from Mom or Dad.

Hear Ye, Hear Ye

Spread family news directly to your grandchild when appropriate—the birth of a new cousin, an upcoming wedding of an aunt, the arrival of a new pet at a relative's home.

Cousin Chatter

Be the grandparent who keeps the cousins close by letting one grandchild know what the other is doing or accomplishing.

Starter Set

Introduce your grandchild to the fun of collecting by beginning a collection of stamps, polished rocks, baseball cards, or mugs for her.

Here's More

Use every opportunity to add to a child's prized collection—whatever it may be.

I Must Tell

Be sure to inform your grandchild of the nice things that people have said about her performances or behavior.

Less Than Twenty Questions

Don't ask too many questions of your grandchild. Wait and listen. Eventually you will get the information you're looking for.

Just You and Me

Create a ritual that is shared by the two of you. It can be a special "high five" greeting, a wink, or a knowing roll of the eyes. Use it every time you visit with your grandchild.

Tycoon

Build a make-believe business together. You'll have much to discuss: What are we selling? Where will we get our materials to make the product? How much will we charge for the product? Where will our office space be? Whom are we hiring? How much will we pay our employees? Suppose you plan to open a circus: What color should the tents be? Who will be the ringmaster? What acts will our circus have? How much will the tickets cost? How many should we keep aside for charities and disadvantaged children?

Leg Lifts

Introduce your grandchild to an exercise routine. Better yet, design an exercise program together.

An Hour More or Less

"*Kid pleasers*" that are fun for you as well as for your grandchild abound. You'll discover—and be surprised by—how much you can do in an hour or two and frequently in just a few minutes. When you're with your grandchild, act as if you have all the time in the world.

Some of these kid pleasers will become standard operating procedure. Many that you introduce to your grandchild will eventually be shared with her children—and grandchildren.

Planted by Pam
Enlist your grandchild's services for any painting, plumbing, or landscaping project you may be doing. She will feel important and proud to have been part of the job.

I Used to Be Good
Play a game of pool or Ping-Pong together.

Back Off
Try not to insist that your grandchild help or do something he would rather not.

Jack and Jill
Keep nursery rhymes, folk songs, and folktales alive by passing them on to the next generation.

I Have Time
Parents never seem to have the time to play board games. Cozy up, relax, and enjoy moving your token around the board.

Set Sail

Build a primitive sailboat from a block of wood and piece of cloth and float it on a nearby pond.

Discovery Mission

Go for walks and point out interesting sights—buildings, people, stores—as you mosey along.

Routine

Add a morning, afternoon, or after-dinner walk with your grandchild to your visiting routine.

Young Guests

Invite your grandchild's friend to stay for lunch or dinner.

Sweet Tooth

If you have one, your grandchild is likely to have one, too. Make a stop together at the candy or ice-cream shop.

Biker's Choice

Set a satisfying destination—a place for breakfast, brunch, lunch, an afternoon snack, or a swim—then head out on bicycles with your grandchild.

Taste Sensations

Acquaint your grandchild with ethnic foods by taking him to Chinese, Indian, Mexican, Thai, Italian, Portuguese . . . restaurants for a change.

What's Cooking?

Stir up some Chinese vegetables, build tacos, or make pasta from scratch in your own kitchen.

Strumming . . .

. . . on the ol' banjo or guitar or ukulele. You can teach her, or she can teach you.

Zebras and Yaks

Go to the zoo together at least once a year.

Sounds Like

Play charades. Pick a category: perhaps fairy tales for younger children, movie titles for the older ones. Teach them the basics, then try to decode each other's clues.

Car Singing

Sing softly to the babies, loudly with the teenagers when you're in the car.

W-R-O-C-K

Listen to the radio station of your grandchild's choice on *your* car radio.

Ice-cream Magic

Turn an ordinary glass of milk into a strawberry float.

Now You See It, Now You Don't

Introduce your grandchild to magic tricks and card tricks you remember. Then show her how to do them.

The Internet

Explore it with your grandchild. Turn yourselves loose on the Information Highway to read about mountain ranges or discover what airlines are offering special rates to a place you both want to go.

Practice Makes Perfect

Request private performances of your grandchild's public "appearances" before and after the show or concert.

Not Bad

Be an honest critic of a speech or role in a play. Offer constructive but positive criticism.

Hole in One

Grandchildren of most ages are always "up" for a round of miniature golf.

Stay!

Attend obedience training classes with your grandchild and his dog.

Roll Over, Fido

Help your grandchild teach his dog tricks.

Beaten

In arm wrestling, your grandchild will be winning before you know it.

Free Tutor

Assist or tutor your grandchild in school subjects you know well.

Grandparents' Day

If your grandchild's school has a Grandparents' Visiting Day, by all means attend if you can.

Spruces, Cedars, and Oaks

Introduce your grandchild to the names of different species of trees, plants, and vegetation.

Apple Pie, Applesauce, Apple Brown Betty

In the fall, locate an orchard open to the public and take your grandchild apple picking. Then have her assist you in transforming the apples into applesauce . . .

Pearly Pink or Fiery Red?

Paint your granddaughter's fingernails and/or toenails in the color she selects.

Main and Fourth Street
Go for a bus ride around town if your grandchild has never ridden a bus.

Free Throw
Teach your grandchild the finer points of basketball out there with him on the court.

Bank Rolls
Sort, count, and wrap the change you've been saving in the bank's special rolls. Your grandchild may deserve a roll of pennies, nickels, or dimes for helping.

Paper Planes
Make them and fly them with your grandchildren.

All Wet
Don your bathing suit and run through the sprinkler with your grandchildren.

The Ways of the World
When paying your bills, teach older children how to write checks and balance a checkbook. They'll be ahead of their class when they learn it in math class.

Pass the Purple Crayon

You may be Grandma/pa Moses. You'll find out when you draw your own or on the same picture with your grandchild.

Celebrate the End of School

Congratulate your grandchild for completing another school year by recognizing his hard work with a token gift such as a sports item for summer fun.

Achievement Award

Another way to celebrate the end of the school year is with a printed award for "Successfully Completing ____ Grade." Printed awards that just need to be filled in can be purchased in many stationery stores . . . or generated on a computer.

Row, Row, Row Your Boat

Each take an oar and row around the lake. Or pretend your house is a lake and "row" from room to room.

Executive Delight

Take your grandchild to your office or job and introduce him to your co-workers.

The Biggest and the Best

Block towers are grandparents' forte. Build them tall and when they fall, build them again.

An Enthusiastic Participant

Get down on the floor and be truly involved in whatever your grandchild is playing. Pointing from a chair doesn't have the same effect.

Beach Creatures

Sand can be molded into fantastic animals—large and small.

Sparrow or Wren?

Binoculars in hand—and a book on bird watching if you need identification help—see how many unusual birds your grandchild can find.

Man the Moat

Since you probably don't have to create sand castles regularly, you can go all out when you do. Spread them out on the beach, add moats to be filled with buckets of water, and find twigs to line paths or crown towers.

Ocean Exploration

Dig for sand crabs, sand dollars, and scallops.

On Shore

Search for unusual seashells and shiny, colorful rocks.

Strike

In all likelihood a grandparent's spare or two at the bowling alley will impress most grandchildren.

Songfest

Sit around the piano and sing your hearts out. Be sure to include your college songs and songs you sang

to your children, so your grandchildren will be able to sing them to *their* children.

Soda Jerk

Teach your grandchildren how to make milk shakes and malts.

Once Around the Park

Ofttimes grandchildren will humor their grandparents. If they agree to take a walk in the park with you and you know that this is not tops on their list, take them up on their good nature. A walk gives you time to talk and get to know one another better.

On the Town

Take your grandchild out to dinner, especially if his parents are out to dinner.

Your Choice, My Choice

Alternate who picks the restaurant for meals out with a grandparent.

Grab Your Partner

If you're like the new generation of grandparents, you're still spunky and spry. Ask your grandchild to dance with you.

Do-si-do

Find a square dance to attend.

Steak for Breakfast

Your grandchild probably shows few signs of being a major athlete yet, but if he wants steak for breakfast or Belgian waffles for dinner, why not? His mother probably won't honor such requests, but you can.

Lemon or Milk?

Turn an afternoon snack into a tea party by serving milk or juice in fancy cups and cookies on a plate.

Sandwich Hero

Be a hero at the cutting board by creating "fancy" sandwiches: cut the bread into triangles, small squares, strips. Use cookie cutters to style the bread. Pile small sections into tottering towers or arrange them in a design on the plate.

Toot Toot

For the grandchild who flies most places she goes, take her on a train ride.

Volume One

Sit on the couch and read together.

Soup's on

Soup and hot chocolate go hand in hand with thoughts of grandparents. Serve your grandchildren soup—it doesn't have to be homemade—and hot chocolate on cold, snowy, and rainy days. Use odd-sized glasses or bowls that your grandchildren may never have seen.

Swinging

Hang a hammock and share it on a hot afternoon.

Trumped

Bridge for older grandchildren; gin, casino, crazy eights for the younger ones. When you discover a card game they love, play it whenever they're around.

One-on-One

Solitaire on the computer or the old-fashioned way is a pastime your grandchild will enjoy learning from you.

Too Messy for Mom

Mothers tire of cleaning up because they do it so often. Grandparents, on the other hand, can easily manage projects that require occasional cleanup. Try your hand at papier-mâché masks or clay pottery

with your grandchild. Finger painting for the younger set is good and messy, too.

What a Lovely Spread

Cover your kitchen table with paper—from a roll, large sheets, or brown grocery bags cut open—and tape down the corners. Depending on age, give your grandchild crayons, paints, markers—whatever is the medium of the moment—and let him draw. Mark off sections so each grandchild has his own space.

Punchy

Colored paper and different-size hole punches will keep a youngster happily engaged in making designs and a mess. Limit this activity to an area that is easy to sweep or vacuum. Outside may be your best bet.

Check It Out

Visit the local library now and then. Check out some books to read to your grandchild.

Privileges

When your grandchild is old enough, take her to sign up for her very own library card.

Stroke and Feather

Canoe paddling is a skill you can pass on to your grandchild.

All Rise

Stop in on the local courthouse to see a courtroom and perhaps a trial in session.

Auto Maintenance

Go together in the car through a car wash or stand off to the side and watch as the car is cranked up on the lift at the garage for an oil change or minor repair.

Root Systems

In a clear plastic cup, plant grass seed or suspend a potato in water. Your grandchild will be able to check the developing root system daily at her home or each time she visits you.

Ever Ready

Purchase a car seat that meets government standards so if you're baby-sitting and the family car is gone, you're free to take your grandchild out whenever you wish.

Over the Weekend

When your grandchild opens the door and you're greeted with a big smile and cheery "Hi, Nana [or Gramps]" or "Hello, Grandma and Grandpa," you know two things instantly: You're glad you came to visit or that your grandchild is visiting you and your grandchild thinks you're wonderful.

Whether the time is spent at yours or your grandchild's home, some preplanning ensures a smooth, fun time for all. Grandchildren have lots to learn from you, and weekends offer unrushed time for many "lessons."

A Space of Her Own

Whether your grandchild visits for a few hours, the afternoon, or the weekend, be sure she has a cabinet, drawer, or a shelf with toys, art supplies, books, and items she can reach without assistance or permission.

Bonus Time

Campaign for overnights. Have your grandchildren spend the night as often as possible. You can count on their jumping in or on your bed, praising your cooking, and having time to get to know you well.

One-on-One

Make each grandchild feel as if she's your only grandchild by taking grandchildren on separate

weekends—or separate excursions—if it can be arranged.

Good Choice

Give up a golf game, a dinner with friends, a weekend away, to be with your grandchildren.

Welcome Mat

It doesn't have to be a floor mat. It could be a special set of glasses, a stack of fancy paper plates, a wading pool, or a toy. Whatever it is, be sure your grandchildren know that it is pulled out only for their visits.

Sleep-over

Reserve a soft blanket and sheets with juvenile designs just for your grandchild's stays.

Revival

Pull out your children's toys that you stored and saved for your grandchildren. The time has come to play with the well-worn dolls, trucks, and trains.

Red or Black

Let her win the checkers game more often than not.

Tub Toys

Keep a supply under your bathroom sink. Add a new one occasionally.

Bang the Drum Softly

A drum set for your grandchild will get you banned from his home. Assuming you can tolerate the noise, keep one in your house.

When the Cat's Away . . .

Parents gone. Now's your chance to supply the treats and surprises grandchildren don't usually have or are not exactly what Mom or Dad think wise.

Baby-sitter's Prerogative

Staying up extra minutes or for one more television show before bedtime will endear you to your grandchild. When you're in charge, it's your call.

Cornucopia

Fill the cupboards and refrigerator with your grandchildren's favorite foods.

Frosted Nuggets

In the supermarket, allow your grandchild to select cereal he likes. Steel yourself for parental protest.

The Lost Art of Cooking

When your grandchildren visit, get out a cookbook and learn or experiment together. Try baking cupcakes or making pudding.

Who Stole the Cookies from the Cookie Jar?

Even if they're not homemade—but better if they are—fill the cookie jar for grandchildren visits.

Place of Honor

Seat your grandchild at the head of the table or in your most comfortable living room chair. The place of honor shows a child just how special he is.

Growing, Growing, Grown

Mark the wall once or twice a year to indicate how much your grandchild has grown.

Hand over Hand

Trace your young grandchild's hand every few months and save each tracing so you can show her how fast she's growing.

Reverse Mechanic

Beginning at ages when you don't have to worry about small parts being ingested, give your grand-

child discarded mechanical or electronic items to take apart—an old telephone, radio, sound speaker . . .

Invasion of Privacy

Examine anthills together with a large magnifying glass.

Flora and Fauna

Explain the trees and flowers in your backyard. They will be different from the vegetation around his house.

Good Tips

Turn your kitchen into a pretend restaurant. Place your order and allow your grandchild to serve you. You may feel inclined to tip your waiter or waitress with a surprise dessert or extra kisses.

For the Ambitious

Build and decorate a dollhouse—a project that can take years.

The Play's the Thing

Frequent the local children's theater together. The first play a child sees is often the most memorable. Bring home the program or playbill. And if you can

arrange to go backstage after the show to meet some of the actors, do so.

Garage Sale

Have a garage or yard sale with your grandchild. He can be a valuable assistant in putting stickers on items, writing prices, manning the money box, and carrying customers' purchases to their cars. Be sure he's paid for his efforts at the end of the day with an item from the sale or in real dollars.

Park Place and Boardwalk

Divulge your strategies for winning Monopoly and other board games.

Short-term Project

Spend the weekend building a model train car, plane, or automobile.

500 Pieces

Assemble jigsaw puzzles with the number of pieces and pictures that match your grandchild's age and ability.

Clipity-Clop

Pony rides are a good introduction to horseback riding.

Versatile Granny

Teach your grandchild to ride a bike, jump rope, or Rollerblade.

Extra Points

Explain football, baseball, or basketball to your grandson or granddaughter while watching a game on television.

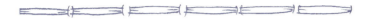

Aces Low

Be remembered as the grandparent who taught his grandchild how to play gin rummy.

Beauty Day

Take your granddaughter to the beauty salon to have her hair and nails "done."

Chocolate Bird's Nests

Welcome spring in a delicious way: Crush four shredded wheat biscuits and mix with four ounces of already melted chocolate chips and one-quarter cup peanut butter. Shape into four nests in the cup of your or your grandchild's hand and chill until set. Fill with jelly bean "eggs."

Show-off

Jump or dive into the pool or lake and show off any water tricks you can still execute safely and successfully.

Go Fish

Send grandchildren who are good swimmers fishing at the bottom of the pool for coins you've tossed in.

Bring a Friend

Allow your grandchild to bring a friend along when she visits.

Morning Paper and Muffins

Invite your grandchild along to the bakery, bagel shop, or newspaper store on Sunday morning.

Odd Animals, Weird Balloons

Pour pancake batter into animal shapes or a bouquet of balloons.

Quack, Quack

If no ordinance prohibits, feed the ducks in the park.

Tennis Anyone?

Be prepared to lose when you take on an older grandchild in a set of tennis.

Listen to This One

Read your grandchild the comic strips he enjoys or listen while he reads them to you.

In the Wind

Go fly a kite—homemade or store-bought.

Bundle Up

Use your years of experience with winter to help your grandchildren create the neighborhood's prize-winning snowman.

Experiments

Find out what's going on at the science museum that would interest your grandchild.

Moon Watch

Witness the slices of the moon appearing night after night until the moon is full.

I Like This One

Plan to learn a new game with your grandchild occasionally when he's visiting or you're visiting him for an extended period.

Just Like Home

Spend time learning her usual bedtime ritual so when your grandchild is visiting, your house seems almost like home.

Dodge City

Use the weekend to create, set up, or play with a train set and city.

A Tree Grows in . . .

Plant a tree in your yard or your grandchild's yard when each grandchild is born. Jeff's tree, Seth's tree, Amy's tree . . . then watch them grow.

Naming Trees

When the child is old enough to understand—or help—buy or make a name sign for his tree.

Cousin Lisa Day

Take your grandchild without his parents to visit aunts and uncles, cousins, and great-aunts and uncles for a day or the weekend.

The Best

Try your hand at candy making.

Camper's Delight

Roast marshmallows in an outdoor fire pit, on the grill, or in the fireplace.

The More the Merrier

Welcome other grandparents and their grandchildren to a barbecue, lunch, or supper with you.

Go Wildcats!

Attend your grandchild's sporting events and be the loudest person cheering.

Congratulations

Comment on sport successes and achievements with an after-event ice cream or pizza.

Play Down Losses

Reinforce good sportsmanship and hard work as you do your grandchild's successes.

Your Grandparents Are Great

Support the team with a basket of apples or oranges or treat team members to hot dogs or ice pops after the competition.

Spinach or Peas

Often vegetable choices are not something a mother offers. Your grandchildren are more apt to eat vegetables if you ask them to select: corn, green beans, or carrots?

Mexican Sundae

Don a sombrero and pour ice cream, chocolate sauce, and a sprinkle of peanuts into a dish with much fanfare. Or wear a cowboy hat and call it a Wild West or Desert Sundae.

Hooked

Introduce your grandchild to fishing. Waiting for the bait to be taken is a good time to talk.

Photo Opportunity

Be sure you take a picture of your grandchild reeling in her first fish or holding it proudly once back on shore.

Nothing Could Be Finer . . .

. . . than cooking up the fish you caught together only a few hours before.

Just Browsing

Stop at a nearby bookstore to learn what subjects

interest your grandchild. This visit will provide you with good ideas for future presents—or perhaps one for right then.

How Do They Do That?

Visit the manufacturing facility of a candy, cupcake, potato chip, or ice-cream company to learn how favorite snack foods are made.

Bottom Drawer

Have a cupboard or drawer that always holds inexpensive gifts–for example, promotional giveaways, bookstore bookmarks, pencils, balloons—little things that you have no use for but that your grandchild will delight in. During each visit, instruct your grandchild to take one surprise from the special cupboard or drawer. After a few visits, she will know the routine.

No Dog

There are other options: lizards, chameleons, turtles, and all their trappings. With grandchild in hand, visit the pet shop. If an aquarium is already in place, have him select an interesting new fish.

Where's Blankie?

Keep extra blankets and key bedtime items at your house for naps and overnight and weekend stays.

Left Behind

Pack up and send off any treasured item your grandchild may have left after a visit with you. Don't hold on to it, thinking she'll come back sooner in order to reclaim the forgotten item.

Waffles or French Toast

Take your grandchild out for weekend breakfast, brunch, or lunch.

Ate It at Grandma's

Introduce your grandchild to new foods—meals and treats he has never tried.

Sowing and Harvesting

Invite your grandchild to help you plant the garden . . . or better yet, harvest the crop—and eat it—if he happens to be visiting for dinner.

Special Delivery

If your grandchild helped you plant the garden but

is not nearby for the harvesting, select some produce and ship it out overnight mail to her.

Pop, Pop, Pop

Plant popping corn this summer; pick it; dry it. Take the kernels off the cob and have your grandchild package them for the freezer. During winter visits, pull out a bag and pop the corn from your garden. (Special popping corn seeds are required; follow instructions.)

Pen, Sock, Key

Send your grandchild through the house to collect ten or so items for you to hide. Once they're hidden, announce in what rooms they can be found. If you're really game, have your grandchild hide the items for you to find. Older children can be timed.

Pitch a Tent

Take your grandchildren camping or pitch a tent in the backyard.

Archeological Dig

Oh, the treasures they'll find in the ground right outside your door. Have grandchildren dig for long lost booty. Borrow their digging spoon or shovel once the hole is a reasonable size and slip pennies just

below the surface for them to unearth when they start to dig again.

Not Too Ripe

Go blueberry or strawberry picking. Once home, turn the berries into jam, jelly, or a pie.

Specialist—Only a Grandparent Can

Only a grandparent can convey some of the family history—events, successes of its members, silliness the grandchild's parents did when they were too young to recall them. And some things only a grandparent can do. Often, you can make promises a parent can't or doesn't want to make.

If something is important to a grandchild, it's important to you. Make your grandchild's dreams come true whenever you can as long as his wishes don't conflict with a parent's rules or values.

A Star Is Born

Attend school plays and music programs whenever possible. Bring flowers to the family's "star" and a camera to record her glorious moments.

Promises Kept

Don't cancel a get-together with your grandchild. You're far more important than you may realize.

Be a Sport

Go ahead, splurge. Buy that irresistible toy, dress, or outrageously expensive pair of sneakers.

Be Extravagant

Don't pass up the chance to indulge your grandchild by giving her computer software.

"Not Another One!"

The parents' cry when you show up with another stuffed animal, as stuffed-animal good fairies are supposed to do.

Holding

Not a football offense and there's no penalty for holding your infant grandchild as often and as long as possible. It's your chance to bond with your child's offspring.

Be Happy

Always be cheerful around your grandchildren. They have parents who can be grumpy and sad.

Sing Their Praises . . .

. . . even if what you say isn't quite accurate. Tell your grandchild you think she's a genius or a world-class ballerina. It doesn't matter that her report card shows nothing but C's and her instructor has made her the stationary tree in the dance recital.

Belt It Out

Sing your favorite songs at the top of your lungs. Your young grandchild will think you should turn professional.

Spare Me

On the other hand, if you can't carry a tune, your grandchild will have a great time teasing you and asking you not to sing.

Extended Babyhood

Allow your grandchild to act younger, perhaps revert back to the bottle or stroller if he wishes when he's with you.

Your Milk, Dear

Part of spoiling includes waiting on grandchildren of all ages.

"No"

"No" is a word that is not in a grandparent's everyday vocabulary. If used at all, it should be used sparingly.

Loving Care

Offer to baby-sit for your grandchild's pets if the family is going on vacation.

The Knitting Basket

If you know how, teach your grandchild to knit, crochet, or needlepoint.

Buy Two

For the grandchild who is "hooked" on a toy or stuffed animal, buy an emergency one, which will save the day should the original fall apart or be lost.

Nite, Teddy

Knit up a sleeping bag(s) for a grandchild's teddy bear and dolls, then help her tuck them in at bedtime. You can fold old diapers or small blankets into sleeping bags as well.

Grandparent Power

Do everything in your power to turn up the scarce item that every child wants and few parents have the time to track down. Take out a phone book, call every store that might have it, and drive those extra miles to purchase it.

I'll Do That

Demonstrate your devotion by doing some of your grandchild's chores for him—make his bed, take out the garbage, set the table, or feed the animals.

Individualism Emphasized

Be known for pointing out the special strengths of each grandchild. Tell each one how impressed you are with a unique ability or strong character trait.

Accessorize

Make or buy area rugs for the dollhouse, tiny lamps and furniture, or other accessories your grandchild's dollhouse may need.

Dinner by Grandmother

Bringing dinner to your grandchildren—complete with their first-choice dessert—once a week or once a month can be very helpful when both parents work.

Food Fads

Whatever food kick your grandchild may be on—chocolate cake, mashed potatoes, milk shakes—make it one you feed. Prepare his preference often.

You're the Funniest

Tell your grandchild you love her wit, her sense of humor. Let her know you think she's very funny.

Buddy System

Challenge your grandchild to a few laps in the pool, a swim out to the raft, or a race around the lake.

Support Every Venture

Always buy what your grandchild is selling—be it Girl Scout cookies, candy bars, magazines, or gift wrap. And buy much more than you would from your neighbor's children or grandchildren.

Organized

Spontaneously take on with your grandchild one of those time-consuming projects, such as cleaning her closet, toy box, or room.

Main Character

Make up stories in which your grandchild is the central character.

He May Be Right

In the face of conflict with his parents, be your grandchild's advocate (but only when it will not cause a huge family war).

For Grandpa, Please?

Some children do not like to have their picture taken. But anything for a grandparent. Keep your camera handy at all times to take pictures of everything involving your grandchild.

Always with You

Carry snapshots of your grandchildren in your wallet. Be sure they know you do.

Who's That?

Bring a snapshot of a distant relative or a happy family event to introduce young grandchildren to distant and often unknown relatives.

Save Your Allowance

Buy your grandchild essentials her parents feel she should purchase with her allowance so she'll have it to spend on things she really wants instead of needs. (Stop if her parents object.)

Never Too Old
Grandchildren never outgrow the fuss you make over them or the happy feeling of hearing from a grandparent.

Back Up
Be your grandchildren's backup day care provider if you're available.

The Whole Family
Display a photo of the entire family, including all the grandchildren if possible, in your living room or office. Individual photographs will accomplish the same goal: they tell your grandchildren they are important enough for you to look at every single day.

Longtime Favorites
Check the same books out of the library that their parent enjoyed. Explain that this was your mother's favorite or that you had to read this one over and over to your grandchild's dad.

Pat the Bunny to *War and Peace*
Cuddle up to read stories and books every chance you get.

Anything Goes

Parents aren't pleased by lengthy periods of silliness, but *you* can tolerate your grandson's less-than-perfect behavior. He'll welcome your attitude and unconditional acceptance.

Be Proud . . .

. . . and say so. You can't say "I'm proud of you" too often.

Just Like Your Mother

Point out similarities between your child and your child's child. Your grandchild will feel very connected when she is told her mother loved to dance too or that she and her father are both good with numbers . . .

A Parent's Job

Leave the tough discipline and training jobs to your grandchild's parents. The children will notice that you're not "on them," too.

The Forbidden

You'll be a champion when you purchase a toy or fulfill a request that your son or daughter refused to meet. Assuming the request is safe and not violently

opposed by his parents, you'll gain lots of points on your grandchild's scorecard.

Room Decoration

His mother's or father's old, probably unusable, baseball mitt or bat is a treasure to a young child and looks great hanging on a bedroom wall or sitting on a shelf.

Go Ahead, Brag

And when you do, be sure your grandchildren hear you. If not, tell them what you said about them and to whom.

Hat Ornament

Have a very small photo—the smallest school portrait size or a baby photo, head only—laminated, add a pin back, and wear it on a cap or sun hat.

Specialty of the House

Barbecue ribs, lemon pie, or a bowl of cereal with a mountain of cut fruit—prepare your specialty for your grandchild. Teach her the secret of the dish—even if it's as simple as putting the fruit on the bottom and the cereal on top so it doesn't get soggy.

Not for the Yard Sale

Ask your grandchildren first—before you relegate their parents' old toys, stuffed animals, and drinking cups to the yard sale table. Keep some of them in the family.

Be the Supplier

Find out what he likes—model cars, computer software, comic books. Hand-deliver or send these treasures. Confer with the child occasionally, as preferences and interests change rapidly.

Shopping Spree

Few things are more exciting than having a grandparent alone in a store. Take your grandchild to her favorite shops and help her make a choice.

The Color of Money

"Green" lights up the eyes of grandchildren old enough to know that this color buys them coveted items and that grandparents part with their green more readily than parents do. Think green, if you can afford to do so.

The Family Dog

Only you can tell your grandchildren stories about their great-grandparent's business, the house you

grew up in, or the funny family dog that opened doors and slept with the cat.

Gift Conference
Call or sit down with your grandchild to solicit his ideas about birthday, anniversary, and holiday gifts for his parents and siblings.

Be the First . . .
Try to be the first to take your grandchildren to the new restaurant in town that caters to kids.

On Display
Use, never store, a grandchild's work of art out of sight. Turn pottery creations into paper clip holders, paperweights, or shelf decoration.

The Good Fairy
That'll be you again. Give your grandchild something on his "wish-to-have" list every so often.

We're Twins
Wear matching baseball caps or sunbonnets.

Not Quite Bedtime
A pre-tuck-in snack is probably not a treat your grandchild gets regularly from his parents. It can be as

simple as a sliced apple or a piece of cinnamon toast cut into triangles. You may prefer to go all out and heat muffins you made earlier in the day or serve ice cream sodas on hot summer evenings.

Redeem Your Coupons

Give grandchildren coupons for goods or your services. "This coupon good for . . ." a chocolate pie, four games of darts, three turns in the front seat, one day building a tree house, a blueberry pancake breakfast . . .

Special Days:
Holidays, Birthdays,
Not-Feeling-Well Days

Most time spent with a grandparent is special, but you can make holidays, birthdays, even days when your grandchildren are not feeling well meaningful and memorable. Anticipate every occasion; approach each one individually and with enthusiasm.

It's never too early to introduce tradition into your grandchildren's lives. During the holidays particularly, you can keep family ritual alive and make celebrations bigger and better than ever before. Your input will raise excitement levels; you'll see young spirits soar.

Stuffing à la Lilly

Give your grandchild a special preparation job for Thanksgiving dinner—mashing the sweet potatoes, mixing the stuffing, stuffing the turkey, whipping the cream, or setting the table. An older grandchild will enjoy the responsibility of stirring the gravy.

To Grandmother's House We Go

Have as many holiday meals as possible at your home.

Be There

Be present at all holiday meals no matter at whose house they are held.

And So We Celebrate
Explain your family's holidays and religious traditions as fully as you can.

A Very Special Day
Arrange one family reunion each year—a day in the summer or fall, on Christmas or Thanksgiving—for as many members of your family as can attend so your grandchild will get to know his relatives.

Your Mother's Favorite
Prepare one holiday dinner dish your daughter or son loved. Let the grandchildren know you served it every Thanksgiving, Christmas, Hanukkah, or Easter, on Washington's Birthday or Valentine's Day.

Light the Lights
Add a day of touring your town with grandchildren to see Christmas decorations.

By the Chimney with Care
Create a Christmas stocking for each of your grandchildren. Knit, crochet, needlepoint, or purchase a special stocking with her name or initials to hang each year.

Stocking #2

Keep second—perhaps smaller—Christmas stockings for grandchildren at your house for them to look forward to when they arrive during the holidays.

Punch It Down

Ask your grandchildren to knead the dough and punch it down for your holiday breads. They'll remember waiting for bread to rise only to take a turn mashing it down again.

Bake-athon

Get in the holiday spirit by devoting a day to baking cookies. Roll the dough, then turn over the Santa, reindeer, star, tree, angel, or Christmas ball cutters to your grandchild. Freeze the cookies for Christmas and Hanukkah celebrations.

Gingerbread People Need a Home

Buy all the fixings and during Christmas week or on Christmas Eve help each grandchild assemble a gingerbread house.

Cookie Art

Ask grandchildren to decorate the cookies and cakes you prepare or teach them how to make their

favorites. Check the baking section of the supermarket for colored sprinkles, "red hots," confetti-shaped sugars, chocolate or peanut butter chips, M & M's, and other candies. Or make your own exotic icing colors by dropping food coloring into your icing recipe.

Personally Crafted

Find directions for baker's clay or salt dough. Kits for making ornaments from paper, wood, and other materials are also available. Assist your grandchildren every year in creating new tree decorations. Save them for use year after year.

Deck the Halls . . .

. . . and the stairways and doorknobs and table legs. Your grandchildren will find plenty of places on which to hang the festive chains of cranberries, popcorn, or construction paper loops you've strung together.

My Way

Give your grandchild a small tree—not necessarily "real"—for his bedroom at home, the kitchen or den, or for the room he sleeps in at your house—that he can decorate any way he chooses.

All I Want for Christmas

Accompany your grandchildren on visits to Santa Claus. Inform them of unusual requests their parents made to Santa.

Dear Santa

Help your grandchild prepare her list and/or write a letter to Santa Claus. Drop the letter in a mailbox together, allowing time for it to reach the North Pole.

Find Yours

Instead of tagging each holiday gift "to" and "from," write—or hide—your grandchildren's initials on the wrapping paper and have them take turns searching for their packages.

Mini Menorahs

Give each grandchild his own menorah so he can select candle colors he likes for every night of Hanukkah.

Stretch the Fun

Extend the eight nights of fun by hiding your grandchild's Hanukkah present each night or on the nights you are together.

Pull Rank

Take full advantage of your age and position when it comes to seating arrangements. Request that your grandchild sit next to or near you.

Where Do I Sit?

Draw or trace (cookie cutters are good guides) Christmas stockings, trees, angels, or whatever your grandchild selects. Cut out one for every person as a place card. Have your grandchild color them, cut them, or write in names and place them around the table. Assist grandchildren in making appropriate place cards for all your dinners.

Jingle Bells Revised

Put family lyrics to a Christmas or Hanukkah song for the grandchildren to perform. Incorporate their ideas, be they silly or sophisticated.

Happy New Year

Wish your grandchildren a happy New Year by phone or in person. Supply party hats and noisemakers. When with them, serve cranberry juice, grape juice, or ginger ale in wine or champagne glasses. Supply a new game or organize a few to play while

waiting to ring in the New Year—which can be done before bedtime, however early that is.

Log Cabin Celebration

For Lincoln's Birthday, you and your grandchild can build a log cabin by gluing pretzel sticks together with peanut butter.

Standing Ovation

When the family's together, gather the grandchildren to write a short play or organize a revue to present to the rest of the family and guests.

Funny Valentine

It doesn't have to be romantic, but sending a Valentine is an opportunity to express your love that you don't want to miss.

Valentines Hand-Delivered

Make heart-shaped sugar cookies with your grandchild. Spread strawberry jam on top and sprinkle with confectioners' sugar. Go together to deliver these eatable Valentines to her friends and relatives.

Candy Hearts

Valentine's Day is a good excuse to give your grandchild chocolate and other candy her parents don't normally permit.

Multicolored Easter

Invite your grandchild's friends to lunch and to experiment with different types of egg dye. Young children can crayon designs before coloring, or paste on stickers when the eggs are dry. Be sure each child goes home with a basket and a few colorful eggs.

Under the Pillow

Jelly beans create a rollicking Easter egg hunt. Even though you give them baskets for collecting, you may

never know who found the most because grandchildren will eat the jelly beans you hide as quickly as they find them.

Note: Put out the dog.

Getting Warmer

Become known as the best Easter egg hider in the business. Discover secret places they'll have fun uncovering. Make a point of either using the same Easter basket each year or changing it every year. Children will come to expect the grandparent basket ritual, whichever you choose.

Latkes and Fried Eel

Holidays are a good time to introduce grandchildren to ethnic food traditions: fried eel on Christmas Eve, plum pudding on Christmas Day, latkes during Hanukkah, corned beef and cabbage on Saint Patrick's Day, hot cross buns during Lent, or Peking duck for the Chinese New Year.

Dazzling

Go out of your way to watch a July Fourth fireworks display. Or create your own celebration by having everyone dress in red, white, and blue. Ask your

grandchildren to parade in a line to march music. Light sparklers after dark.

Red, White, and Blue

Arrange a Fourth of July barbecue or picnic with neighbors and friends (yours or your children's). In keeping with the day, serve patriotic food: red—watermelon, cherries, red grapes, red peppers, radishes; white—bread, rice, mashed potatoes, cream cheese; and blue—blueberries, blue corn chips, blueberry jam, for example. For dessert, have angel food cake topped with vanilla ice cream and strawberries and blueberries.

Patriotism on Display

Send small flags for your grandchildren's rooms or to wave at a parade. Consider supplying red, white, and blue streamers for decorating their bicycles to ride in a neighborhood Fourth of July parade.

Always on the Job

Pick up canes, hats, jackets, magic wands, sports equipment, even complete costumes, at yard sales and garage sales during the year. Nothing has to be the right size for right now.

Bring Outside Inside

Cover your kitchen floor with leaves for Halloween festivities, trying on costumes, or carving pumpkins. Be sure to roast the pumpkin seeds.

Be Picky

Be the annual pumpkin provider. Take grandchildren out into a country field to select their own pumpkins if there's a farm nearby. If not, let parents know that you're supplying the Halloween pumpkins each year. Be choosy; the larger, the better.

Pumpkin Faces

For or with your grandchildren, make a dessert of canned peach halves, using cottage cheese for hair, chocolate chips or cloves for eyes, nose, and mouth.

Red Nose, Black Whiskers

Save your almost-used-up lipsticks, eyebrow pencils, eye shadows, and powders for grandchildren to apply instead of masks.

Plaid Shirt and Large Shoes

Give or send your grandchild old clothing, boots, shoes, and hats for her Halloween scarecrows.

Witches, Goblins, and Oreos

Make or supply your grandchild's costume or part of it each year. Cut holes for arms and head in a pillowcase; draw an Oreo cookie on front and back. Complete the outfit with white gloves and white painted face. Or send two children off as M & M's by drawing an orange candy on one pillowcase, green on

another. Paint their faces to match the candy colors, and remind "M & M" to stay together.

Queen for a Day

One is never too old to get into the swing of Halloween. Don a mask or paint your face to prove you are young at heart.

Down to Business

Give your grandchildren large trick-or-treat collection containers. Decorate old pillowcases with Magic Marker designs or purchase orange and black bags or baskets. Plastic pumpkins with handles also do the trick.

Trick or Treat

Accompany younger grandchildren as they make the rounds, then sort through the candy with them.

Best Leaf Raker

Present Grandparent Awards annually when the whole family is together. Make up categories: "best company," "best kisser," "best jumper," "best climber". . . Have the award be significant and always flattering.

Happy *Birth* Day Party

When taking a grandchild to see his newborn sibling, prepare for a hospital party by bringing cupcakes, paper plates, party hats, napkins, and a gift for your grandchild to give his new sister or brother. Ask permission to light a candle in one cupcake. Be sure to sing and take pictures.

Happy Birthday Creations

Assist your grandchild in making gifts and cards for his parents, sisters, and brothers. Add homemade get-well greetings to your do-it-together list.

Supplier

Buy your grandchild a special dress or suit or tie for special occasions in a special store.

Good Excuse

Birthdays are good for being excessive. Give what you can and make the celebrant feel important. Include young siblings by giving them a small gift, too.

Happy Birthday

A telephone call first thing on the birthday morning is a must.

Personalizing

Store-bought birthday and holiday cards can be individualized by snipping your grandchild's head from an extra photograph and attaching it on top of a figure, cake, or drawing on the card.

Make a Wish

Turn an ordinary cake into an eye-opener quickly by placing animal crackers on the sides between the

icing lines you've drawn to resemble a tent. Ice sliced cupcakes in different colors and position them on top of the cake to look like a cluster of carnival balloons. Hold the "balloons" together with licorice strings. And use tube icings to write your grandchild's name.

Couldn't Be There
Send balloons or flowers for the birthday parties you miss.

Lowdown
Call after a grandchild's party to find out what happened and to talk about the gifts he received.

A Family Affair
Make or take your grandchild and her parents, brothers, and sisters out for a special birthday lunch or dinner.

Special Birthdays
Different birthdays are considered more important in different families and cultures. For some it's a thirteenth birthday, sweet sixteen, or a Communion year. For your grandchild's significant birthdays, select gifts that he or she will have for many years—a necklace, a watch, a clock, a radio . . .

Bells Are Ringing

Present your grandchildren with a special bell to ring when they are sick and can't get out of bed.

Bedside Manner

Should your grandchild be hospitalized, visit or call every day if you can.

Good Company

Rent a video for the young patient and stay to watch it with him. Watch a television show, read, or sit quietly in the room. It's a good time to delight in the joy of being a grandparent.

Encouragement Needed

Keep reassuring the young patient that she will be better.

Pampering

A definite "must do" for grandparents of sick grandchildren. Bring in lots of little, quiet activities— materials to make potholders, beads, or felt art, simple model kits, and books that encourage bed rest. Wrap surprises as you would a birthday gift.

Very Tempting

Freeze juices into ice pop animals and unusual shapes. Special forms are sold in most supermarkets.

On Call

Try to pitch in when your grandchild is ill by taking a shift or spending a few days in the house. Stay with your grandchild all night if the situation calls for vigilance.

Almost as Good as Mom

You're the next best thing to having his mother care for him. It's comforting to have a grandparent close by, reminding the patient that this is the way you took care of his mother/father.

All-Occasion Grandparent

Be it a sick day, holiday, birthday, Columbus Day, or other occasion, give your grandchild's parents a small gift—wrapped, of course—from you to place on the floor of her bedroom. It will be the first thing she sees when she wakes up.

Little Things Mean A Lot

Little things tie you to your grandchildren, and them to you and to other members of the family. You are the supplier of happy memories to treasure throughout life—be it your comforting hug and kiss, a fantastic made-up story, or your unending praise.

Because so much of what a grandparent does involves giving, there will be times you (or your grandchild's parents) may want to take the emphasis off gifts. More often than not, it is the simplest, least expensive amusement or gesture that forms the most lasting impression: a grandparent who peels an apple in one unbroken strip, who listens when you have a problem, who plays cards with you for hours on end.

When grandchildren are young, some of the small things you do for them and with them seem insignificant, but those things are the very ones that turn into family legacies in the years ahead. With these ideas you will be creating a warm history for your grandchildren and giving them a lifetime of love . . . and loving you.

Modigliani, Definitely

Take the masterpieces out to be professionally framed . . . or frame them yourself. A framed picture is a great gift for your son or daughter for hanging in their home so the child can see it every day. It's a constant reminder that the family thinks his work is exceptional.

You'll Know a Classic When You See It

Ask your grandchild to save you or send you selections of her artwork. She'll feel proud and you can show off her talent by hanging the work in your home or office. Let her know that's what you've done.

Budding Artist

Build or buy an easel, keep it stocked with paper and drawing supplies, and encourage the artistic leanings in your grandchild.

For the Fish

Supply equipment for the tank, a rock for the lizard, instead of a gift that's directly for the child.

Spotlight the Dog

Bring the dog a box of bones or a colorful bandanna.

For Your Mother

Bring a gift just for his mom.

For Mom, for Dad

Offer your grandchild your shopping services and advice when it's time to buy presents for her parents.

Arf, Woof, Bark

Ask parents if you can be the one to give your grandchild his first dog.

Dachshund or Great Dane

Spend time studying different breeds of dogs before your grandchild selects her puppy. Consider puppy shopping at the local animal shelter. You may find the perfect family dog there.

I Scream, You Scream, We All Scream . . .

When the ice-cream or ices truck comes down the street, give your grandchild money to buy him-self—and you—a cooling snack from the ice-cream man.

Leonard Bernstein, Surely

If you can't take your grandchild to his extracurric-ular instruction, perhaps you'll want to foot the bill or part of it.

A Little Encouragement

Encourage your grandchild to attempt more than he thinks he can, then tell him how phenomenal a job he did or how courageous he was.

Tick Tock

Grandfathers give grandfather clocks—large and small. There will never be a question as to who gave that gift.

Country Classics

Have grandchildren participate in traditions and rituals from your country of origin so that they can pass them on to their children.

Baby Feet

"My foot was that small!" That's what your grandchildren will say when they look at the baby shoes you had preserved in bronze or porcelain.

U.S. in Postcards

Grandparents who travel can acquaint their grandchildren with the country by sending postcards from different states they visit. Ask your friends who live in other parts of the country to mail postcards from their home states directly to your grandchild.

Beach Bums

Comb the beach together for treasures early in the morning. Save some of them in a special box or container.

Photoplay

Turn extra photos of family events and trips into postcards and mail them to your grandchildren. Photo supply stores have backings to do this.

Picture Perfect

Teach your grandchild how to use a camera. Start him off with a disposable camera pack.

Smile, Everyone

Encourage your grandchild to use the videocamera. Teach her the basics of getting in close on her subject and framing her composition.

Sorting

Spend some time sorting or looking over your grandchild's baseball or basketball card collection. Dazzle him with sport statistics if you know them.

Treasure Chest

A special privilege kept in a "secret" place. For visits to your house, store a pretty container or old jewelry box chock-full of junk jewelry. You can purchase inexpensive beads, pins, earrings, and bracelets at fairs and flea markets, yard and garage sales. Relinquish a trinket every so often.

Precious Jewels

Provide your granddaughter's first jewelry box and give her an heirloom to put in it.

In Charge

Put your grandchild in charge frequently. Have her call to make reservations or to check movie schedules. Give her money to pay the check at a restaurant or to buy tickets at the movie theater.

Growing Up

Give your grandson his first razor.

Measuring Spoons and Potholders

Buy your grandchild's first cookbook.

Correspondence Course

Order your grandchild return address labels or stickers with her name on them.

Build a Collection

Start a collection for a grandchild of mugs, spoons, T-shirts, or magnets from places you visit.

Don't Touch

A fabulous series of collector dolls that you may not want your grandchild to play with now becomes treasured when she's old enough to understand the beauty, uniqueness, and value of each doll.

Grandparents Unite

Invite one of your grandchild's friends and *her* grandparent to join you for a movie, a carnival, or another special outing. Save ticket stubs, programs, or souvenirs.

One Outfit . . .

. . . handmade by you—it could even be a sweater or scarf for her best doll—is enough to be cherished and remembered for a lifetime by your grandchild.

A Penny Saved . . .

Open your grandchild's first bank account. The initial deposit amount is not what's significant.

Matching Funds

Have your grandchild give or mail you money she's saved, earned, or been given. Let her know you will add a matching amount and deposit it in her account. Fifty-cent pieces and dollar bills accumulate substantially over the growing years.

For the Future

Buy your grandchild's first bond.

Stockbroker in the Making

Buy your grandchild a share or two—a comic book stock, food stock, computer stock—then show him how to follow it on the stock market pages in the newspaper or on the computer. Your range of choices of stocks selling for one dollar or less is enormous.

Just Water

Give your grandchild a hearty plant to nurture and show her how to nurse it.

"Andrea" in Green

Attention grandparents who can needlepoint: Design a pillow with your grandchild's name on it.

Start Now

Knit or crochet an afghan for your grandchild's room. Too busy? Start soon so it will be ready for her to take to college.

Tee Off

A round of golf—especially the first one—goes hundreds of feet in the memory department.

For Starters

Yes, this year and every year, provide your grandchild with a new pencil holder, book bag, backpack, highlighters, or colored pencils to start a new grade.

Assignment Book

If you're lucky enough to be asked to shop with your grandchild for school supplies, turn the time

into a special event by ending with lunch or an extra treat.

Changing Faces

Keep school photos on the refrigerator, on a bulletin board, in view somewhere. Or reserve a frame just for school photos and replace the old one every year. Keeping photos up-to-date shows a grandchild you truly care.

Sleepy Time

Surprise your grandson with a new set of bed sheets and a fluffy comforter for his room.

Bath Time

Order a special towel set with her name imprinted.

Take Me Out to the Ball Game

Ask to take your grandchild to his first major league baseball game—or at the least, ask to go along with the family to one.

Attention-Getter

If you're computer savvy, design different stationery for letters and notes you send. Add your grandson's name to pictures or symbols of his favorite

foods or sport. One figure in the corner of a page can make the page unique to him.

Rhinestones and Rubies

Pin one of your old brooches to your grand-daughter's jacket, coat, or hat. Give her a necklace or bracelet you no longer wear.

No Confusion

Order your grandchild pencils or pens with her name on them.

Memo to Grandpa

"Thank you for the pads with my name. They are on my desk. Love, Chris."

Personalized stationery with envelopes for letter writing is another gift that will be recalled years later.

Mini-memories

One thing about grandparents, they help keep film companies in business. Put the best pictures of events, trips, or a day's outing you've enjoyed together into small, individual albums to look at with your grandchildren when they visit.

Music, Maestro, Please

Introduce your grandchildren to music by taking them to a children's concert.

Marching Bands and Ferris Wheels

Pick a parade, fair, or flea market and take your grandchild every year.

Daredevil

Muster up the nerve and get on the amusement park ride with your grandchild that his parent refuses to attempt.

Old Softy

Get a reputation for always giving in to your grandchild.

Was the Tooth Fairy Here?

Find a tiny pillow or make one to hold those missing baby teeth. Your grandchild will use it, then put it away for her children.

By Jamie Donaldson

Write a book together. Spread the writing over several visits (this project can take months) and illustrate it with your grandchild's art or photographs you take together. Be sure to have it bound. Make a few copies for your grandchild to distribute as he wishes.

The Piano, the Candlesticks

Leave something—your priceless miniature antique cars, a painting, a piece of jewelry, an old radio, your garden tools, a back scratcher, shoehorn, or

worn-out hand fan—to each grandchild. Spell it out in your will.

The Recording Type

Log family gatherings and memorable events, especially those revolving around the grandchildren, in a notebook, in pictures, or on videotape. Give your chronicle to your grandchildren, who can pass it on to theirs as a permanent record of little things long remembered—and proof that little things really do mean a lot.

Top Priority

When you keep your grandchildren foremost in your mind, they always know you value them.